THE PRIVILEGED PLAYER

A METAPHOR FOR HOW THE REAL-WORLD WORKS
AND HOW TO SUCCEED IN IT

FELIPE REYES

Copyright © 2024 by Felipe Reyes.

All rights reserved.

No part of this book may be used or reproduced in any form whatsoever without written permission except in the case of brief quotations in critical articles or reviews.

Printed in the United States of America.

For more information, or to book an event, visit:
http://www.privilegedplayer.com/

Book Design by Felipe Reyes and Ultimate Book Formatting
Cover Design by Felipe Reyes

ISBN: 9798322533733

First Edition: May 2024

The views, thoughts, and opinions expressed in this story belong solely to the author, and not necessarily to the author's employer, organization, committee, or other group or individual.

This story is for informational purposes only and should not be taken as financial advice. The author is not a financial advisor, broker, or dealer.

The content of this story is intended to share the author's personal investing journey and strategies for the future benefit of his heirs. Investments and strategies mentioned in the story are personal to the author and may not be suitable for all readers. Readers should not construe the information provided as a recommendation to buy or sell securities or to adopt a particular investment strategy.

Investing involves risk including the potential loss of principal. Past performance is not indicative of future results. Readers are advised to conduct their own independent research and consult a professional financial advisor before making any financial decisions. The author and publisher of this story shall not be liable for any errors or omissions in the content, or for any actions taken in reliance thereon.

This story may contain forward-looking statements which are based on the author's current expectations and projections about future events. These statements are not guarantees of future performance and involve risks and uncertainties that are difficult to predict.

By reading this story, you acknowledge and agree that you are doing so at your own risk and discretion and that neither the author nor any affiliated parties will be held responsible for any financial losses or gains experienced.

CONTENTS

How did we get here? ... 9

THE GAME

1. THE PRIVILEGED PLAYER ... 15
2. THE DISADVANTAGED PLAYER ... 19
3. THE MILLENNIAL PLAYER ... 21
4. GENERATIONAL WEALTH ... 23
5. RIGGING THE GAME ... 25

THE GAME PLAN

6. THE TRANSITIONAL GENERATION ... 31
7. BECOMING THE PRIVILEGED PLAYER ... 33
8. THE FUTURE VALUE OF MONEY ... 37
9. THE HERO'S JOURNEY ... 49
   Star Wars: A New Hope ... 51

Conclusion ... 57
About the Author ... 59
References ... 61

For Auggie.

*And for all the working people
who struggle to make ends meet.*

HOW DID WE GET HERE?

Our world looks vastly different today compared to when I grew up in the 1970s and 80s. TikTok is full of videos of young people talking about how previous generations were able to afford college and a house, all on one salary! I remember my friend's parents owning small businesses, like an auto-parts store, a barber shop, a news stand, a pizza parlor, and a printing business. They were upper middle class. They had Disney vacations every other year, nice clothes, new cars, a lake house. Those small businesses are now gone, replaced by corporations. College tuition is expensive, home prices are out of reach for many, and wages are stagnant. Prospering with one paycheck is no longer possible. People are now in survival mode.

What happened? How did we get here?

There are many complex issues that economists, sociologists, politicians, academics, and business leaders can point to that explain our current situation. Depending on which business cycle we're in, whether it's a boom or a bust, the news never quite fits our personal experience. The headlines might say that the recession is over or maybe it just started, inflation is under control or not, and unemployment is at an all-time low but you still can't find a job. Whatever the economic conditions might be, many people are still struggling to make ends meet. What's the disconnect?

Sometimes, to understand a complex issue, you have to simplify it. You have to "unpack" the situation, peel away the layers, and get to the root cause. I like to use metaphors to make sense of things. This story is a metaphor for how the real-world works. Is it an oversimplification? Yes. But it's a short and simple story that will help you understand our world, get you thinking, and, hopefully, empower you to seek more information, and make some adjustments, so you can move from surviving to prospering.

This book is not meant for the MBAs with a firm grasp of the theories behind finances, economics, statistics, and an understanding of the *Capital Asset Pricing Model*. This book is for the server who is a single mother, working double shifts to make rent, and not seeing the light at the end of the tunnel. It's for the over-the-road truck driver sleeping in his cab at the truck stop, away from his family for weeks at a time. It's for the first-generation college graduate from a working-class family who took the advice, got a degree, yet is still struggling because the promise of the prosperity from a corporate job never quite materialized. And college debt is burying them before they even begin.

I've told *The Privileged Player* story many times to family and friends. It wasn't until I heard Rick Rubin[1], the famous music producer responsible for hits by Tom Petty, Mick Jagger, and The Red Hot Chili Peppers, say that when you're creating something, you're creating it for yourself. Since you're just creating it for yourself it's not for anyone else to tell you if it's good or bad, right or wrong. Think of it as a journal entry. No one can say that your journal entry is wrong.

I'm writing this story for myself, hopefully you'll find it useful too.

 Throughout the story you will see a key takeaway icon. This serves as a bookmark to help you go back and quickly reference important material.

THE GAME

1

THE PRIVILEGED PLAYER

In 2014, psychology professor Paul Piff[1] from the University of California - Irvine, conducted a series of experiments on narcissism. One of his experiments involved rigging a game of Monopoly where a coin was flipped to determine who would be the "Rich Player" and who would be the Regular Player. The rich player received more of everything that a Regular Player would normally get. For example, the rich player collected $200 when passing *"Go"*, whereas the Regular Player collected $100. At every turn the rich player reaped outsized rewards. It wasn't long before the rich player started acting differently and attributed their wins to their superior intellect and skill. The reality was that the only reason the rich player was winning was because he won the lucky coin toss. It's like being born on third base and thinking you hit a triple.

The first time I heard about this experiment I was intrigued and wanted to perform my own experiment. At the time my son was very young so we tried the same thing but with Chutes and Ladders. We didn't flip a coin, I just let him be the rich player. Sure enough, my boy started winning and was visibly excited that he was beating dad. We moved up to Monopoly when he got a little older and this time, we actually flipped a coin. Sometimes he would be, what I came to call *"The Privileged Player"* and sometimes it would be me. It was interesting to see how he behaved when he was a Regular Player versus when he was privileged. Professor Piff's experiment has been done countless times in our household, with the same results every time. The Privileged Player takes credit for winning the game, and yes, he would win every time.

This experiment works on just about any game. If it's a foot race to the corner you can flip a coin and assign a Privileged Player who gets a 30-foot head start. Guess who wins? Or, you're hitting a piñata at a birthday party, flip a coin, assign the Privileged Player who doesn't have to wear a blindfold. The Privileged Player always wins.

The circumstances we are born into is just luck. Like flipping the coin to see who will be the Privileged Player during our board games.

As my son and I continued using the Privileged Player concept, I thought that this is a good metaphor for how the world actually works. But the game needed more representation if this was to be an accurate metaphor, so I expanded on Professor Piff's experiment and added new players.

2

THE DISADVANTAGED PLAYER

So far, with the flip of a coin the *Privileged Player* is assigned. Flip another coin and the *Disadvantaged Player* is assigned. For this role, the player gets **less** of everything.

The Regular Player gets $1,500 at the start of Monopoly, the Privileged Player gets $3,000, and the Disadvantaged Player gets $750. The Disadvantaged Player gets fewer dice and less money when they pass "Go". It doesn't take long for the Disadvantaged Player to become frustrated. They can't seem to catch a break, they can't afford to buy anything, they don't get equal amounts of money on spaces that call for it. At some point a Disadvantaged Player says the game is rigged. The thing is, the rules haven't changed. It's just that each player; the Privileged Player, the Regular Player, and the Disadvantaged Player, all have different levels of resources, so their experiences on the game board are vastly different. And it was all based on the flip of a coin.

The Disadvantaged Player resonated with me because I've struggled to make ends meet. It's difficult to try your best but still fall short. The typical advice I've gotten to get out of this situation is to work harder or work smarter. I've thought to myself that maybe I'm just lazy, or stupid. But the truth is that I was dealt the Disadvantaged Player card so I had fewer resources. There is no one to blame, it is what it is. Being "Disadvantaged" is subjective, I know. What one person deems a disadvantage, another person might be looking at them and wish they had the same advantages. It's up to each of us to determine which player we are, and which player we aspire to be.

3

THE MILLENNIAL PLAYER

So far, we've introduced the Privileged Player and the Disadvantaged Player to the game. Both were based on a coin flip. There is another player joining the game, the *Millennial Player*. As with the other players, this player is also determined with a coin flip.

The Millennial Player gets the same resources as a Regular Player, but they are also burdened with student debt[1] that needs to be paid to the bank on regular intervals. I included a rule that student loan payments are due at every roll of the dice. Also, to remain true to the Millennial experience, you can't discharge your student loan debt if you are declared bankrupt (in Monopoly). The Millennial player, with his funds dwindling at every roll of the dice, has access to fewer assets on the board.

Once again, the game is not rigged, the rules have not changed. The only difference is how the resources and debts are assigned. And like the Disadvantaged Player, the Millennial Player becomes frustrated with the game, and a certain amount of animosity is directed towards the Privileged Player, while the Regular Player just tries to hang on.

4

GENERATIONAL WEALTH

So far, the Privileged Player, the Disadvantaged Player, and the Millennial Player have joined the Regular Player on the game board. But our metaphor isn't complete yet. There are other factors in place that we need to consider, most notably Generational Wealth. By far the most impactful element of the game.

When the game is over and all the other players have cashed out, the Privileged Player retains all of his winnings. He hangs onto the cash, the properties, everything. When a new game is played everyone starts at zero, but not the Privileged Player. He has all the resources from the previous game. This allows him to take advantage of more opportunities and perhaps acquire even more assets.

This new element of the game is not too far from the truth. The heirs of many robber barons of the 1800's created The Gilded Age, thanks to the generational wealth created by their forefathers. You can trace the wealth of today's 1%, at least in part, to generational wealth[1].

The Privileged Player, with the help of the coin toss, and generational wealth, acquires more assets and wins over and over again while the rest of the players become disheartened. But the Privileged Player has one more trick up his sleeve.

5

RIGGING THE GAME

There's one more wrinkle in the game that will make our metaphor complete. All the players are on the board. The Regular Player is trying to hang on. The Millennial Player is loaded with debt. The Disadvantaged Player can't afford anything. And the Privileged Player has more assets, more opportunities and generational wealth to dominate the game.

Now, the Privileged Player begins using that vast wealth and resources to change the rules in their favor. If you land on *Luxury Tax*, all players must pay, with an exception for the Privileged Player. *Free Parking*? Not anymore. All players must pay, except of course for the Privileged Player. You can see where this is going. Money buys influence. Let's look at a real-world example.

In my opinion, the government should be the keeper of the rules in the economy. We're supposed to have a government that represents the people and acts as a referee to ensure the game is played on a level playing field, where hard work is rewarded, and ingenuity and intelligence helps you get ahead. It's my belief that is what *"To Promote the General Welfare"* means in the US Constitution.

Unfortunately, that's not the case anymore, if it ever was. A study conducted by Princeton University[1] found that regardless of how popular an initiative was with the public, Congress only acted on it about 30% of the time. If 90% of the people wanted something done, there was a 30% chance Congress would do it. If 20% of the population wanted something done there was also a 30% chance Congress would act.

However, when it came to issues, laws, and initiatives that special interests wanted, it seemed to track the level of support. If 90% of corporations wanted something done, there was a 90% chance that Congress would get it done.

Economists have a saying that there is an "invisible hand" that moves the economy. That invisible hand has a name, it's ALEC, the American Legislative Exchange Council[2]. This is an organization consisting of elected officials and private sector corporations that draft legislation that becomes law. Coupled with the fact that Citizens United[3] allows corporations and wealthy donors to donate money to campaigns anonymously and leverage political influence, it's no wonder that special interests get what they want.

I'd like to make a distinction between government and elected officials. I'm not referring to the hard-working people that make our country run. I'm referring to **some** elected officials from both parties that use the system to their advantage.

Back to our story. When new players were added to the game the only differences were the resources each player had, but the rules stayed the same. The non-Privileged Players may have complained that the game was rigged, but it really wasn't. However, **now the game is actually rigged**.

I think the story of the Privileged Player is an accurate metaphor for what we are currently experiencing as a society.

With a flip of the coin the Privileged Player gets more resources, creates generational wealth, then uses that wealth to rig the system. Meanwhile the Regular Player, the Disadvantaged Player, and the Millennial Player slowly get pushed off the board. Sound familiar?

I've shared this story with family and friends, and it would always come across as gloom and doom. I started thinking, how can someone become the Privileged Player if they didn't win the coin toss?

The good news is that there is a path for future generations to become the Privileged Player. It requires a *Transitional Generation*.

THE GAME PLAN

6

THE TRANSITIONAL GENERATION

I've always been interested in how some people succeeded so brilliantly, like Cornelious Vanderbilt[1], Henry Ford[2], and other titans of industry. As I read their biographies, I saw a trend. They all had a mentor, someone that would guide and advise them and was truly interested in helping them succeed.

Vanderbilt had Thomas Gibbons[3], a wealthy southern landowner that used his vast fortune after the revolutionary war to invest in the latest technology, steam engines. Henry Ford had Thomas Edison[4] as a mentor. He actually built his first car while working as an engineer for Edison Illuminating Company in Detroit. They all started out as Regular Players.

Steve Jobs[5] also had a mentor, it was Mike Markkula[6].

Mike Markkula worked at Intel in the marketing department when it was private. He made out handsomely when it went public. When he was looking for a new opportunity, he was referred to Steve Jobs by Nolan Bushnell, the founder of Atari where Jobs used to work. When Mike arrived at the now famous Los Altos garage[7] where Apple was housed, he saw the potential in the Apple computer. Markkula was the first investor in Apple putting up $250,000 as an angel investor. He used his MBA and experience at Intel to create the very first Apple business plan, and he was one of the first board members. Mike Markkula mentored Steve Jobs and was the driving force in the early days of Apple.

I never had a mentor. When I was younger, I sought them out, I was always turned down. I believed I would be further along in life if I had had a mentor. After reading the Steve Jobs biography by Walter Isaacson[8], something clicked in me…maybe I wasn't meant to be "Steve Jobs", maybe I was meant to be Mike Markkula, seeing the potential and helping the next generation succeed. This led me to think of myself as the *Transitional Generation*.

In the context of this story, the transitional generation is someone that thinks about future generations and sets things up so that their heirs can **become** the Privileged Player in the future.

7

BECOMING THE PRIVILEGED PLAYER

What I am about to share with you is not financial advice. I am not a licensed financial professional. **Please refer to the financial disclaimer located in the beginning of this book.** I'm merely sharing what I figured out and what I'm doing to make sure my son, grandkids, and generations to come are hopefully Privileged Players in the future.

I grew up in a world of scarcity. Coming from a large working-class family it was normal to economize as much as possible. Orange juice was rationed, clothes was worn until they basically fell apart. We weren't poor, just working class. When I started working and earning my first few paychecks, I wanted to buy all the things I couldn't have when I was younger. I would buy nicer clothes, go on vacations, and buy a better car that wouldn't break down at the most inappropriate time. There are deep psychological reasons why I needed to go on a spending spree to fill the void, this is something I'm not qualified to address, but I think this was just a stage in my life that I had to go through.

I was also unaware of investing and how to manage money. Eventually I got to a point in my life where I began to understand the importance of investing, putting money away in a 401K, and buying a mutual fund, but it was too late for generational wealth for myself.

If you grew up in scarcity you might have also gone through the same cycle of buying things you didn't have growing up. This may lead to investing later in life, if at all. You might build a nest egg that will serve you in your retirement, but it's not generational wealth. You might use up all those funds in retirement, leaving very little for your heirs.

I thought that it might be too late for me to generate generational wealth for myself, but as the transitional generation it wasn't too late for me to start investing for my son. I realized I had time.

TIME IS YOUR BIGGEST ASSET!

Consider the future value of money. If someone were to invest $100 per month from age 40 until they retired at age 65, they would have $185,000 (assuming an average rate of return of 11% which was the historical average over the last 50-years for the S&P 500)[1].

If they are 30 years old and want to retire at age 65, that same $100 per month nets them $625,000. That's $440,000 more. Ten years makes a big difference.

What if someone is the transitional generation? By thinking about their kids, they can potentially make a dramatic impact. If they're struggling and don't have $100 extra every month, they can consider a smaller dollar amount, remember, time is their biggest asset, so a smaller dollar amount is OK. If their child is 12 years old, and they invest $25 per month until the child is 65, that's $1.3 million. At $50 per month that's $2.6 million by age 65.

Let's say a grandparent is considering the future of their grandchild. If the grandparent were to invest $25 per month from birth until the grandchild is age 65, that grandchild would have $5.4 million! Maybe the grandparent makes a few changes to their spending habits so they can increase the investment from $25 per month to $100 per month, that's **$21.9 million by the time the grandchild is 65**! That's life changing and can be the foundation of generational wealth for their family.

A grandparent may have to pass the investment responsibility to the next generation once they're gone, but at least they've gotten the family started on the path towards generational wealth.

It only takes one person in a family lineage to set future generations on a new course. Being the transitional generation takes sacrifice, but the benefits are amazing.

8

THE FUTURE VALUE OF MONEY

To quote the famous investor and billionaire Warren Buffett… "*Time is your friend, impulse is your enemy*"[1]; and Albert Einstein is said to have called "*the power of compound interest the most powerful force in the universe.*"[2]

They're talking about the future value of money. This is a concept that the super wealthy understand. We need to understand it as well.

I needed a way to quickly calculate the future value of a purchase at the moment when the impulse buy was about to happen, so I created an app called the *Future Value App*, it helps me see the true cost of an item. I use it before making a large or recurring purchase.

The following are a few examples.

Suppose I want to buy a TV for $800. Using my Future Value App, I enter my son's current age (12), the age he may want to retire (65), and the dollar amount of the purchase. This is a one-time purchase so there are no monthly payments. The future value of $800 over 53 years is over $416,000.

Do I really need a $416,000 television? Am I sacrificing my kids and grandkids futures? I think twice before making that purchase.

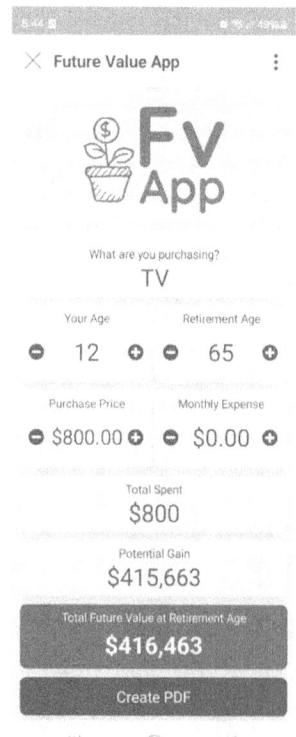

Another way of using the Future Value App is to see the financial impact some of your habits are costing you.

If you are 25 years old and you buy a $5 power bar every day, the future value of that habit could be up to $1.6 million by the time you are 65.

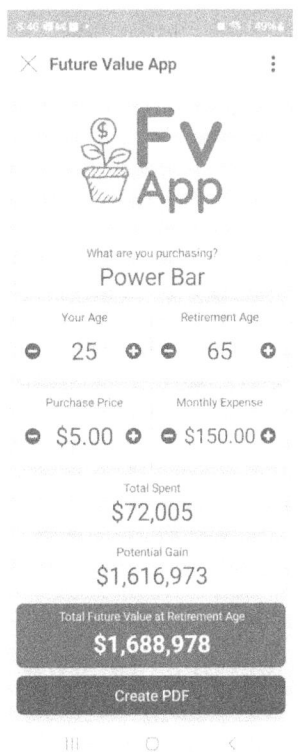

Buying lunch every day at $18 each time, the future value could reach $4 million by age 65.

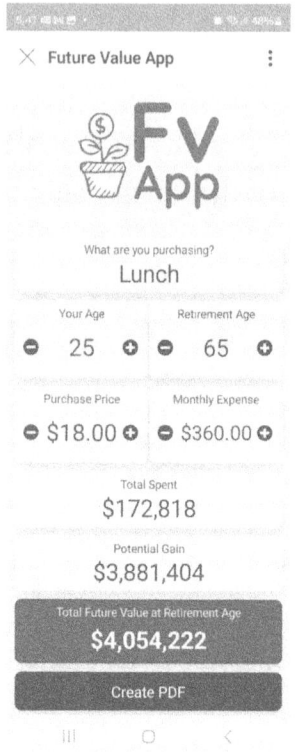

 You might not be spending this dollar amount each month forever, but **if you develop the habit of spending you can develop the habit of saving and investing.**

It's unrealistic to expect a total elimination of a lifestyle choice. Quality of life should also be considered, with allowances for certain indulgences. But if you consider making choices that cost 50% less, you can free up cash that can be repurposed towards generational wealth.

 There is no guarantee that an investment will grow. But there is a guarantee that the buying power of a dollar will decrease over time[3], it's called inflation[4]. Gas used to cost $1 per gallon and you could buy a house for $80,000. Those days are gone, inflation has set in. Look at the buying power of a dollar as a moving platform, if you stand still, you'll be left behind. You have to move at the pace of the platform to keep up, and move faster than the platform to get ahead.

There are many financial instruments that may help money keep pace with or exceed the rate of inflation. I started with a low-cost index fund.

What is a low-cost index fund? According to CNN,

"Low-cost index funds are an inexpensive way for people to build a diversified investment portfolio. These funds are suitable for both new and experienced investors, and the best low-cost index funds allow you to meet your investment goals while aligning with your risk tolerance and investment time horizon"[5].

 In layman's terms, an index fund is a basket of stocks made up of the top 500 companies in the US. Imagine a stock portfolio made up of 500 Michael Jordans. If one of them starts to under-

perform, it is taken out and replaced with another Michael Jordan.

Warren Buffet, the famous billionaire had this to say regarding investing in index funds.

"The average person will not know enough to know which stocks to buy. They won't know enough to know when to buy them. But they don't have to because they can buy all of America through an index fund. And then they just have to be sure they don't jump in at exactly the wrong time. And they won't know what is exactly the wrong time. So therefore, they should put their money in over a period of time and they'll have some periods that are wonderful, and some that weren't so good, but overall, they will do fine over time." [6]

Some S&P 500 Index Funds with the lowest fees are:

- Fidelity 500 Index Fund (FXAIX)[7] – 0.015% fee
- Vanguard 500 Index Fund ETF (VOO)[8] – 0.03% fee
- Schwab S&P 500 Index Fund (SWPPX)[9] – 0.02% fee
- T. Rowe Price Equity Index Fund (PREIX)[10] – 0.20% fee

There are other index funds available, please do your own research.

By the way, the letters next to each fund are the tickers, which is how they are identified on the stock exchange. I chose FXAIX in a Fidelity Custodial Brokerage Account for my son.

A *Custodial Brokerage Account* is an account set up by an adult for a child that allows you to buy stocks, bonds and other assets without the need for a stock broker. Once the child turns 18, they have access to those funds. There are a lot of nuances to consider. Maybe you can convert the brokerage account to a Roth IRA after the child starts working so it's growing tax free. You also have to think about tax and legal implications. I encourage you to look further into it if this is the route you'd like to go.

I see a low-cost index fund as a safety net. My boy will no doubt set up his own retirement plan when he gets older, and possibly have more sophisticated investments, but the fund I set up will add to his advantages. The $100 per month that I invest for my 12-year-old will be worth $5.3 million by the time he's 65. If he starts with $100 per month at 25 years old, he'll net $1.1 million. That's a $4.2 million difference. **Remember...time is your biggest asset**!

BEWARE OF THE DOLDRUMS!

At first, the index fund will grow slowly. In the first 10-15 years you might not see much growth; you may even see a decline or a loss. This is what I call the doldrums, where it feels like not much is happening. This is the point where some people get discouraged and consider buying other high-flying assets, or even worse, cashing out. It's the classic Tortoise and the Hare story[11]. You have to keep at it and get past the doldrums[12], a period of inactivity of stagnation.

In the example below you'll see that if someone were to cash out after 25-years they would lose out on all the future growth. The last 10-20 years is where the most of the growth will come from.

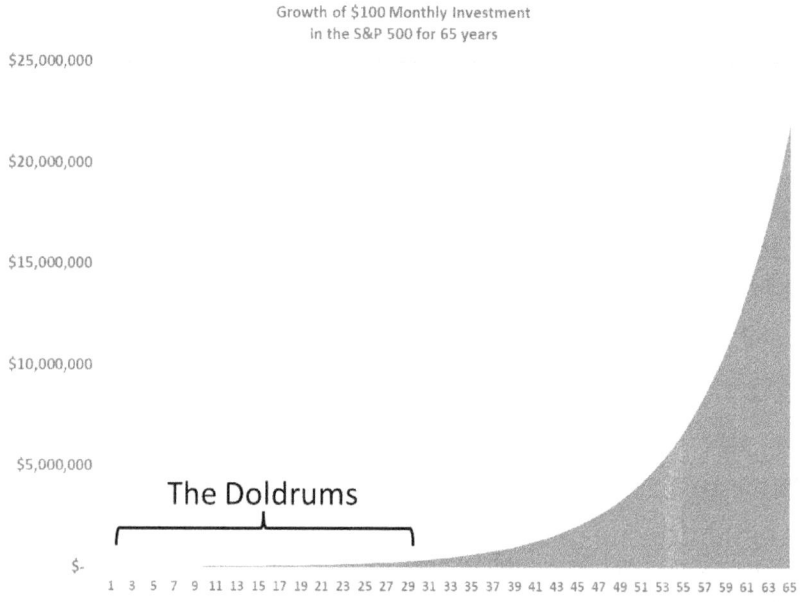

If someone is 30 years old in Year 1, they might not see any significant growth begin until they are 60 years old. But, if Year 1 of the fund is when a child is born, that child will see significant growth start when they are in their late 20s or early 30s. This might motivate them to stay the course into their late 50s and 60s.

Imagine, if opening up an index fund for a new born was considered something you just naturally did, like buying diapers, setting up the crib, or buying baby clothes.

Let's see an example of what that might look like.

At $100 per month, the child has $75,000 by age 18.
At 30 its $342,000.
At 40 its $1.1 million.
At 50 its $3.7 million.
At 60 its $12.1 million.
By age 65 its $21.9 million!

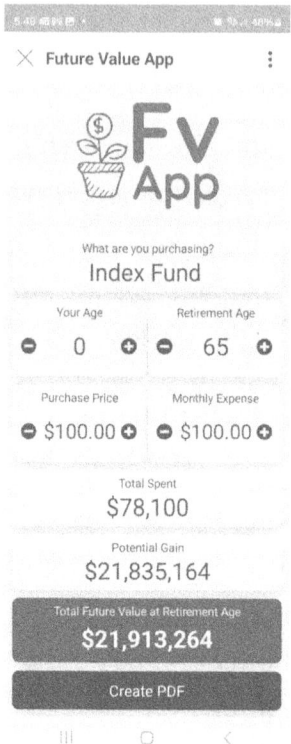

$21 million by the time they're 65! Sounds too good to be true. I based my calculations on the average returns of the S&P 500 over the last 50 years. There is no guarantee that the trend will continue. Maybe only a fraction of that return will materialize. Lets take a look at probabilities.

If I'm wrong, and you only get 10% of what the projection says, then you'll get $2 million. Not bad for a $100 per month investment. The actual returns are somewhere within the range below.

Probability	Initial Investment	Potential Gain	Total Return
100%	$78,100	$21,821,900	$21,900,000
90%	$78,100	$19,631,900	$19,710,000
80%	$78,100	$17,441,900	$17,520,000
70%	$78,100	$15,251,90	$15,330,000
60%	$78,100	$13,061,900	$13,140,000
50%	$78,100	$10,871,900	$10,950,000
40%	$78,100	$8,681,900	$8,760,000
30%	$78,100	$6,491,900	$6,570,000
20%	$78,100	$4,301,900	$4,380,000
10%	$78,100	$2,111,900	$2,190,000

KEY TAKEAWAY

Regardless of when you started or what the actual returns may be, don't get discouraged. Stay disciplined, keep the monthly investments flowing, and fight the urge to cash it out. And when you hear business leaders say that they are working to maximize shareholder value, they are talking about you as well.

There are so many choices when it comes to investing that sometimes people feel overwhelmed. I'm sure there will be plenty of readers that will say that I failed to mention Bonds,

Sector Mutual Funds, Crypto Currency, Real Estate, the list goes on and on. I chose the easiest and least expensive option as a foundation.

Investment choices feel almost like when the personal computer first came out (yes, I'm that old). There were so many choices that, some people, including myself, wanted to wait until the latest technology came out. That day would never come because new technology was always coming out. Eventually I bought a PC, to the dismay of my Apple friends. It didn't matter, I had a computer and I was "in the game". Eventually I learned more and upgraded accordingly. Investing kind of feels the same way. Pick something to start with and evolve from there.

Hopefully this chapter gave you a new way of looking at money, time, and the way time is your biggest asset when investing. I encourage you to seek out more information and start your generational wealth journey to help your future generations become the Privileged Player.

9

THE HERO'S JOURNEY

A good story is memorable.

I had a friend, an older gentleman, that was a huge history buff. He would always quiz me on all kinds of historical facts. Once he asked me if I knew the name of the ship that delivered the atomic bombs that were dropped on Hiroshima and Nagasaki. He quickly followed up and said, not the plane, the Enola Gay, but the naval ship. I said YES! The USS Indianapolis. He was shocked. He then asked if I knew what happened to the ship after they dropped off their payload. I said YES! It was hit by a torpedo and sunk, and half the crew was eaten by sharks. He was amazed. He asked how I knew that; I told him I had learned about it from the movie Jaws. It had easily been 25 years since I had last seen Jaws, but the scene on the boat, where Quint tells the story of the Indianapolis[1], stuck with me. A good story is memorable.

Hollywood uses a formula to tell a good story, it's called *The Hero's Journey*[2]. It's been around for a long time and just about every Hollywood movie follows the same formula. It's a cycle, think of it as a clock.

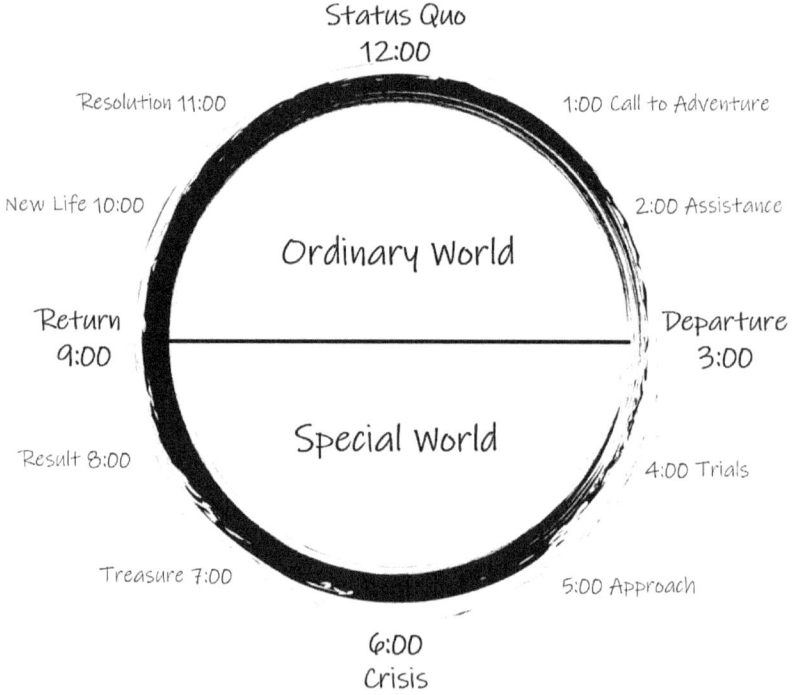

The hero moves from the ordinary world to the special world, dealing with obstacles and adversity until they achieve their goal and return transformed. I'll give you an example.

STAR WARS: A NEW HOPE

12:00: Status Quo Our hero lives in the ordinary world.	Luke Skywalker is a farm boy on Tatooine.
1:00: Call to Adventure The hero is called upon to take on a challenge.	Luke sees the hologram message from Princess Leia asking for help.
2:00: Assistance The hero needs help.	Luke gets help from Obi-Wan Kenobi.
3:00: Departure The hero leaves the ordinary worlds and enters the special world.	Luke leaves his home and sets off to rescue the princess with Han Solo aboard the Millenium Falcon.
4:00: Trials Our Hero overcomes challenges.	Luke is having a difficult time using the force, but with the help of Obi-Wan he begins to master the power.
5:00: Approach The hero faces his worst fear.	After escaping the trash compactor on the death star, Luke sees him mentor, Obi-Wan, killed by Darth Vader.
6:00: Crisis This is the hero's most difficult moment.	Screaming down the trench in his X-Wing Fighter, Luke can't hit the target.

7:00: Treasure The hero overcomes the crisis and gets the treasure.	Luke turns off his computer and uses *The Force*, and the torpedo goes in.
8:00: Result The hero achieves what they were after.	Luke pulls up and away as the Death Star explodes behind him.
9:00: Return The hero returns to the ordinary world.	Luke returns to a hero's welcome and is awarded a medal by Princes Leia.
10:00: New Life The hero has been transformed.	Luke no longer dreams of being a fighter pilot, he is one.
11:00: Resolution The hero's life gets back on track after the journey.	Luke isn't going back to the farm; he is now part of the rebellion.
12:00: Status Quo The cycle starts again but our hero has been transformed.	But eventually, *The Empire Strikes Back*, and Luke is off on another call to adventure.

KEY TAKEAWAY

I think we can sum up the journey to becoming the Privileged Player using the same formula.

12:00: Status Quo Our hero lives in the ordinary world.	This is your life as a Regular Player, Disadvantaged Player or Millennial Player.
1:00: Call to Adventure The hero is called upon to take on a challenge.	It's this story that motivates you to start your journey to becoming the Privileged Player.
2:00: Assistance The hero needs help.	You begin to research some of the index funds I highlighted. Or you use the Future Value App to see what your spending habits are costing you.
3:00: Departure The hero leaves the ordinary worlds and enters the special world.	This is the moment you change your mindset and consider yourself the transitional generation and become an investor.
4:00: Trials Our Hero overcomes challenges.	It's difficult for you to find additional money to buy an index fund. But by using the Future Value App and making a few buying behavioral changes you are able to find the money.

5:00: Approach The hero faces his worst fear.	For you this might be the fear of possibly losing your money in the stock market. This is understandable, since opportunities look like risk at the moment. It isn't until later that they look like opportunities.
6:00: Crisis This is the hero's most difficult moment.	You had a family emergency and you need money. You have to fight the urge to cash out your index fund.
7:00: Treasure The hero overcomes the crisis and gets the treasure.	You fought the urge to cash out the index fund, and your nest egg continues to grow.
8:00: Result The hero achieves what they were after.	You stayed the course, diligently invested money for your kids, and when they reach retirement age, they have generational wealth.
9:00: Return The hero returns to the ordinary world.	You have become the investor class. Entering a new world of possibilities.
10:00: New Life The hero has been transformed.	Thanks to you, your family has become the Privileged Player.

11:00: Resolution The hero's life gets back on track after the journey.	For you this is the moment when you can begin to withdraw funds from the index fund. And possibly begin using some of those funds to invest in future generations.
12:00: Status Quo The cycle starts again but our hero has been transformed.	Your new status quo is Privileged Player.

And the cycle starts all over again with the next generation.

CONCLUSION

In the first half of the book, I shared a metaphor that explains how the Privileged Player gets ahead while the Regular Player, the Disadvantaged Player, and the Millennial Player fight to stay on the game board.

In the second half I shared how thinking of myself as the transitional generation, using the Future Value App to see the true cost of a purchase, and knowing that time is my biggest asset, I can work towards positioning future generations as The Privileged Player.

There are still major issues in our economy like stagnant wages, high tuition costs and skyrocketing home prices. There's not much we can do about that. But there are some things that we **can** do.

It used to be that the American Dream could be attained through hard work. That's no longer the case. But the dream is still alive, and if you play the game right you can still reach it. In addition to hard work, you have to become the transitional generation and invest in future generations by taking advantage of time, compound interest and the future value of money.

You can also begin to think how you want to participate in the economy by modifying your buying habits and redirecting money to assets that will benefit you in the future.

I hope this story has given you a new perspective and inspired you to begin your journey to becoming *The Privileged Player*.

Visit www.privilegedplayer.com to download the **Future Value App** and access other resources.

ABOUT THE AUTHOR

Felipe Reyes is a father and a business professional with over 25 years of experience working in corporations and nonprofit organizations in sales, marketing, operations, and general management roles.

He earned an MBA from the University of Illinois Urbana-Champaign. He lives in Oak Park, Illinois with his son Auggie.

REFERENCES

Preface

[1] Lewis Howes. (2024, March 15). *Access Your Creative Mind*. YouTube.

https://www.youtube.com/watch?v=IVe9-_ebyXk

Chapter 1

[1] Brancaccio, D., & Conlon, R. (2021, January 19). *Why rich people tend to think they deserve their money.* Marketplace. https://www.marketplace.org/2021/01/19/why-rich-people-tend-think-they-deserve-their-money/

Chapter 3

[1] Whittle, W. (n.d.). *Millennials and student loans: Rising debts and disparities.* New America. https://www.newamerica.org/millennials/reports/emerging-millennial-wealth-gap/millennials-and-student-loans-rising-debts-and-disparities/

Chapter 4

[1] Malacrino, D. (2020, November 30). How the rich get richer. *IMF Blog.* https://www.imf.org/en/Blogs/Articles/2020/11/30/how-the-rich-get-richer

Chapter 5

[1] (2004, August). *Inequality and Democratic Responsiveness: Who Gets What They Want from Government?* Gilens, Martin; Princeton University, Politics Department.

https://www.princeton.edu/~mgilens/idr.pdf

[2] ALEC Exposed. (n.d.) *Through ALEC, Global Corporations Are Scheming to Rewrite YOUR Rights and Boost THEIR Revenue.* https://www.alecexposed.org/wiki/ALEC_Exposed

[3] Federal Election Commission. (2020, February). *Citizens United v. FEC.* Federal Election Commission United States of America. https://www.fec.gov/legal-resources/court-cases/citizens-united-v-fec/

Chapter 6

[1] Wikipedia. (2024, February 19). *Cornelius Vanderbilt*. Wikipedia. https://en.wikipedia.org/wiki/Cornelius_Vanderbilt

[2] Wikipedia. (2024, March 7). *Henry Ford*. Wikipedia. https://en.wikipedia.org/wiki/Henry_Ford

[3] Stiles, T.J. (2009, April 21) *The First Tycoon: The Epic Life of Cornelius Vanderbilt*. ISBN 978-0375415425. https://en.wikipedia.org/wiki/The_First_Tycoon

[4] The Henry Ford, (n.d.). *Edison and Ford: A Lasting Friendship*

https://www.thehenryford.org/collections-and-research/digital-collections/expert-sets/101111/#:https://www.thehenryford.org/collections-and-research/digital-collections/expert-sets/101111/#:~:text=Thomas%20Edison%20was%20both%20a,reality%20was%20quite%20the%20opposite.

[5] Piccotti, T. (2023, May 22). *Steve Jobs*. Biography. https://www.biography.com/business-leaders/steve-jobs

[6] Om, A. (2023, July 2). *Steve Jobs, Mike Markkula, and the power of surrender*. Medium. https://medium.com/sd-wisdom-at-work/steve-jobs-mike-markkula-and-the-power-of-surrender-cc562a1a2d78

[7] Atlas Obscura. (n.d.) *The Apple garage.* Atlas Obscura. https://www.atlasobscura.com/places/apple-garage

[8] Isaacson, W. (2011, October 24). *Steve Jobs.* Simon & Schuster.

https://en.wikipedia.org/wiki/Steve_Jobs_(book)

Chapter 7

[1] Mitchel, C. (2024, January 8). *Historical average stock market returns for S&P 500 (5-year to 150-year averages).* TradeThatSwing. https://tradethatswing.com/average-historical-stock-market-returns-for-sp-500-5-year-up-to-150-year-averages/

Chapter 8

[1] Inc. Magazine. (2023, August 25). *5 Pieces of Money Advice Warren Buffett Gives Millennials That Everyone Else Should Follow Too.*

https://www.inc.com/minda-zetlin/5-pieces-of-money-advice-warren-buffett-gives-millennials-that-everyone-else-should-follow-too.html

[2] CBS News. Roth, Allen (2011, June 7). *Compound Interest – The Most Powerful Force in the Universe.*

https://www.cbsnews.com/news/compound-interest-the-most-powerful-force-in-the-universe/

[3] U.S. Bureau of Labor Statistics. (2023, February 9). *Consumer price index: Purchasing power and constant dollars.* U.S. Bureau of Labor Statistics.

https://www.bls.gov/cpi/factsheets/purchasing-power-constant-dollars.htm

[4] Oner, C. (n.d.) *Inflation: Prices on the Rise.* International Monetary Fund. https://www.imf.org/en/Publications/fandd/issues/Series/Back-to-Basics/Inflation

[5] Carlson, Debbie; Curcio, Paul; Tony, David. (2024, January 30). *What are low-cost index funds?*

https://www.cnn.com/cnn-underscored/money/low-cost-index-funds#:https://www.cnn.com/cnn-underscored/money/low-cost-index-funds#:~:text=Low%2Dcost%20index%20funds%20are,tolerance%20and%20investment%20time%20horizon.

[6] Buffett, Warren. (n.d.) *Investing Advice.*

https://www.dropbox.com/scl/fi/gkctwn2hfby6smd3it8pk/52def9604d4c7a6e00131c5fa0ba76b1.mp4?rlkey=0mfk3bxc6to78z8l8jutoby6s&dl=0

[7] Fidelity 500 Index Fund (FXAIX). https://fundresearch.fidelity.com/mutual-funds/summary/315911750

[8] Vanguard S&P 500 ETF (VOO). https://investor.vanguard.com/investment-products/etfs/profile/voo

[9] Schwab S&P 500 Index Fund (SWPPX). https://www.schwabassetmanagement.com/products/swppx

[10] T. ROWE PRICE Equity Index Fund (PREIX). https://www.troweprice.com/personal-investing/tools/fund-research/PREIX?src=USIFundRedirect&adobe_mc_sdid=SDID%3D35D9353AF33B1668-582B7BCAF1A51FA9%7CMCORGID%3DD15D15F354F647770A4C98A4%40AdobeOrg%7CTS%3D1707070667&adobe_mc_ref=https%3A%2F%2Fwww.google.com%2F

[11] Wikipedia. (2024, February 24). *The Tortoise and the Hare*. Wikipedia.https://en.wikipedia.org/wiki/The_Tortoise_and_the_Hare

[12] Merriam-Webster. (n.d.). *The Doldrums Definition*. Plural, Noun.

https://www.merriam-webster.com/dictionary/doldrums

Chapter 9

[1] Rotten Tomatoes Movie Clips [Movieclips]. (2011, May 28). *Jaws (1975) - The Indianapolis Speech Scene* [Video]. YouTube. https://www.youtube.com/watch?v=u9S41Kplsbs&t=1s

[2] TED-ED. Winkler, Matthew. (2012, December). What Makes a Hero. https://www.ted.com/talks/matthew_winkler_what_makes_a_hero?language=en

www.ingramcontent.com/pod-product-compliance
Lightning Source LLC
Chambersburg PA
CBHW070412230526
45471CB00006B/2774